DOCKLANDS
LIGHT RAIL

Official Handbook

Alan Pearce

Brian Hardy

Colin Stannard

Capital Transport

Fourth edition 2000

ISBN 185414 223 2

Published by Capital Transport Publishing
38 Long Elmes, Harrow Weald, Middlesex

Printed by CS Graphics, Singapore

Photographic credits

Ian Bell 55

Capital Transport 1, 3, 16, 17, 19, 20, 21, 22, 23, 24, 25, 26, 27, 28, 29, 30, 31 Top, 32, 33, 35 Top, 36, 37, 38, 39, 41, 43, 45 Top, 45 Bottom, 46, 47, 48, 49, 50, 51, 53, 54, 56, 57, 58, 59, 60, 61, 62, 64, 70, 73

DLR 13, 18, 34, 35 Bottom

Brian Morrison 31 Centre, 44, 45 Centre

Alan Pearce 4, 9, 10, 11, 14, 15, 65, 69

Contents

Property development occurred on a large scale early on in the DLR's history. This view is between Crossharbour and Mudchute.

Origins of the DLR

The closure of London's up-river docks had left the capital with an area of about 8½ square miles suffering all the signs of urban dereliction; the jobs had gone or moved downstream to container handling ports like Tilbury, public transport had declined and social, retail and leisure facilities had either gone or had not kept pace with the type, quantity and quality appearing elsewhere in London.

In 1972, the London Docklands Study Team commissioned Travers Morgan & Partners to investigate and report on ideas for the redevelopment of the area. Whilst the report, published in January 1973, saw a future demand for better public transport to serve the Isle of Dogs peninsula, this was thought to be insufficient to justify a new conventional railway, let alone an Underground line. Instead, a low cost 'minitram' peoplemover system with vehicles carrying up to 20 people each was seen as the answer to connect Docklands with the proposed Fleet Line at Fenchurch Street.

In 1974 the Docklands Joint Committee was formed by the Greater London Council, along with the Boroughs of Greenwich, Lewisham, Newham, Southwark and Tower Hamlets. Its object was to develop Docklands as quickly as possible, with a combination of new industry and housing. The committee reviewed the existing state of local public transport and examined the possibilities for improvement to suit the needs of the new development. Two light rail options were considered, one terminating at Tower Hill (District and Circle Lines interchange) and the other at Fenchurch Street (proposed Fleet Line interchange), but both were considered too expensive.

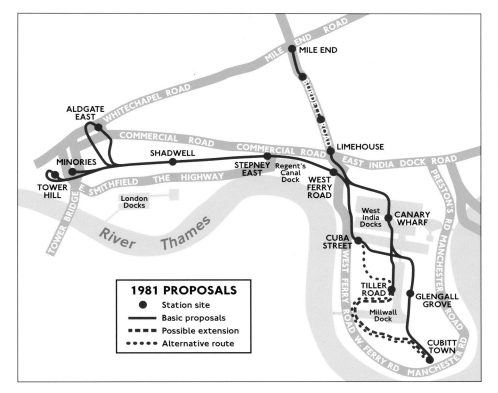

A London Transport study of 1981 of light rail options for Docklands. A line to Beckton had appeared in a map produced the previous year and was to be revived in 1982. Street running is included to Mile End and a short tube tunnel loop terminus at Aldgate East or Tower Hill. Conversion of the East London Line to light rail was also listed as a possibility.

A 1976 report recommended early construction of an Underground line to serve the area and parliamentary powers were obtained by London Transport for a tube connection from Charing Cross via Fenchurch Street, Surrey Docks, Isle of Dogs, North Greenwich and Custom House to Woolwich Arsenal.

However, things changed rapidly and radically when Margaret Thatcher's Conservative government took office on 4th May 1979. As early as June of that year, Norman Fowler as the new Minister of Transport put the brakes on commitment to the construction of a tube through or near Docklands for reasons of financial restraint. The government insisted that a review of lower cost options for Docklands be undertaken.

Most of the options looked at were not new, but a most significant development was a recommendation to check out the feasibility of a fully segregated automatic light rail system from Aldgate East to the Isle of Dogs and on to Beckton.

A plan drawn up as a result of this envisaged 13 stations on a 13 km double-track line, 1 km of which was to be in tube at the Aldgate end, and a depot at Beckton. It was the formation of the London Docklands Development Corporation (LDDC) in July 1981 that was to inject new urgency into the need for a decision. Soon after the LDDC was formed, it commissioned London Transport to study ways of introducing a low-cost rail-based solution to satisfy the needs of the development. The main alignment options examined in this 1981 study are shown in the map above; all were light rail.

A desirable answer would have been to link a light rail metro into either the District/Metropolitan at Aldgate East or somewhere further east, or the District/Circle at Tower Hill, to connect Docklands directly with a multiplicity of central area destinations. It soon became clear that capacity problems on the existing train paths would not permit light rail trains joining the system at any of those points. There was the possibility of using the East London Line in the Docklands solution, but this in itself was effectively divorced from the rest of the Underground for the same reasons. Because direct integration of the new line into the main system looked impossible, there was therefore no reason to make the new facility compatible with the existing Underground network.

One of the simplest options viewed for the east/west line was to install street tramway from Aldgate East all along the Commercial Road to Limehouse. A variant was to use a central alignment along The Highway on the level, which could have been at least segregated from the street, although how this would lock into the scheme east of Limehouse was uncertain.

Three possible city termini were viewed, although a low level interchange beside the existing Underground station at Tower Hill was ruled out at an early stage because it would have been very costly to construct in such a way as to avoid undue congestion. The two more feasible alternatives were a low level interchange station at Aldgate East or a high level terminus at Minories. It was the latter that eventually became the Tower Gateway terminus of the DLR.

It made sense to adapt the existing BR viaduct from Fenchurch Street to what was then called Stepney East Station (today Limehouse). BR had indicated that their utilisation of the viaduct could be pruned to two tracks apart from the immediate approach to Fenchurch Street Station. Therefore a new section of viaduct would be needed from Cannon Street Road into the new elevated Minories terminus. If the Tower Hill option had been feasible, a 5% ramp to tunnels would have started from Cannon Street Road leading to a loop about 10 metres below the District/Circle platforms. Escalators would have led up to these platforms and the existing exit would have been shared between Underground and light rail passengers. Likewise, if Aldgate East had been the terminus, the ramp to tunnels would have started at Cannon Street Road, leading to a loop with a single platform at some 90 degrees to and 13 metres beneath the District/Hammersmith & City platforms. Exit to the street would have been via the Underground platform and either existing ticket hall.

Eastward from Stepney East, the disused London & Blackwall railway viaduct beckoned. On the Isle of Dogs two possibilities existed – a 'western' route running across Millwall Docks Cut to Cubitt Town, or a 'central' route right down the middle of the peninsula, dependent on the West India Docks being infilled or bridged. The 'western' route would have left the London & Blackwall viaduct immediately east of West Ferry Road to more or less parallel that road southwards before turning eastwards to pick up the line of the old dock railway to serve a station at Cuba Street. From there, Millwall Dock cut could have been crossed by a lifting bridge, with a light rail station placed at East Ferry Road/Glengall Grove. A terminus was planned for Manchester Road, Cubitt Town, reached by reuse of the derelict viaduct following refurbishment.

The 'central' route was more or less what materialised into today's DLR, crossing the West India Docks from north to south, with a station planned at Canary Wharf. On this location, the report says '... if extensive dock filling takes place, this could provide a good location. Otherwise it would be very isolated with poor traffic prospects'. Extension across Millwall Outer Dock to Cubitt Town did not feature in this proposal and the terminus was to be sited at Tiller Road. However, in its manifestation as the DLR, the 'central' route turned east before reaching Millwall to adopt the southern part of the 'western' alignment, crossing Manchester Road to terminate at Island Gardens.

The north-south route had originally been put forward as a fall-back option to provide a basic rail connection into Docklands if the direct east-west option proved to be too expensive. However, in the light of the LDDC population and employment forecasts, and in the absence of any direct connection to the south of the river, it became clear that the north-south route was needed as well as and not instead of the east-west one. For the north-south line, a street tramway was also a possibility, with trams running from close to Mile End Station along Burdett Road to Limehouse, East India Dock Road, and then onto West India Dock Road, from which point the north-south route would move onto segregated track to share whatever alignment was eventually selected for the east-west line on the Isle of Dogs.

With both these outline schemes, there remained scope for extension at a later stage off the east side of the Isle of Dogs towards the Royal Docks and Beckton, where stage 2 of the Docklands regeneration programme was planned.

A final report, jointly prepared by the GLC, LDDC, DTp, DoE, DoI and LT, was issued in June 1982. It recommended the construction of two light rail lines comprising a 'west-south' route from the City to the Isle of Dogs, and a 'north-south' route from Mile End Station to the Isle of Dogs. Within three months, government funding was promised for the Docklands Light Railway.

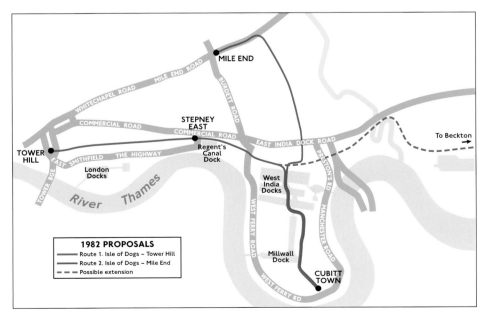

Somewhat unusually, funding was authorised before a Parliamentary Bill had been deposited. This was provided jointly by the Department of Transport and the Department of the Environment, on the strict understanding that the total of £77m not be exceeded and that the project be completed by 1987. Funding came with a remit to take full advantage of existing technology, yet to avoid technical solutions which might compromise the target cost or opening date, or compromise reliable and economic operation. Furthermore, the completed railway was to be operationally self-sufficient, with no revenue support promised by government.

Initial Royal Assent was granted in April 1984, the delay being partly caused by the 1983 General Election, and partly by an unresolved Parliamentary petition during passage of the Bill through the House of Lords.

In the meantime, a very significant alteration was made to plans for the Mile End section of the second route. The climate was not yet right for the Highway Authority to accept street running along part of the very busy A11, Mile End Road. This proved to be convenient for the LDDC which was keen to see a high-tech automated system in place, and this could only be possible if the entire route were to be fully segregated. This desire also over-rode proposals which considered using the wide Burdett Road from Mile End to Limehouse, a much less busy thoroughfare than the Mile End Road, which could have met with the approval of the London Borough of Tower Hamlets, especially if a segregated crossing of the Commercial Road could have been created at Limehouse.

The alternative alignment took the line further north along the railway cutting beyond Bow before climbing steeply and suddenly eastwards to parallel the main East Anglia railway on embankment to terminate instead at a disused bay platform at Stratford Station. The DLR would therefore not serve Mile End, although the interchange facilities with other modes afforded at Stratford were undoubtedly more comprehensive, and it was actually a better traffic objective in its own right than Mile End would have been. A second DLR Bill reflected this change before being deposited in November 1983, with Royal Assent granted in April 1985.

The original intention was to invite tenders based on engineers' designs and specification in the time honoured way, and place one contract for mechanical and electrical engineering, and another for civil engineering works. Following direction from government in mid-1984, it was decided to invite tenders for a single design and construct contract for the entire railway, with tenderers free to offer equivalent alternatives to the basic specification.

In August 1984, a contract was placed with GEC-Mowlem. Now that the railway was to utilise a fully segregated alignment, the offer of automatic train operation that came as part of the GEC-Mowlem package could be accepted

Until the era of the large-scale development proposals for the Isle of Dogs (from mid-1986 onwards), the DLR was expected to actually have to look for traffic and customers, rather than as has happened since, to at times have an embarrassment of business. Thus, the planning assumed relatively low hourly figures to move – 1,500 initially, per hour per direction. This capacity level resulted in a planned timetable of eight departures per hour on each of the two legs of the initial Railway,

combining to give a more impressive 16 trains per hour serving the combined section of route on the Isle of Dogs. It was to meet this part of the Performance Specification that the tendering parties bid in 1984 and it was this simple timetable that the railway used for its pre-marketing. However, what had seemed attractive, and indeed almost too good to be true to some local residents in 1984, proved to be an embarrassment by the time the railway was actually ready to carry passengers a mere three years later.

Planning work to upgrade the system began before the public opening in 1987. Simply put, the planners required the railway to be rebuilt with a remodelled main junction at Poplar and with longer platforms to accept two-unit trains. The trains were to be run more frequently with an improved signalling system and with more operational flexibility provided by reversing facilities at Crossharbour and a passing loop at Pudding Mill Lane. The railway company at the same time was required to run a passenger service to meet the expectations of the growing workforce and the local residents who had long been promised better public transport.

Above left **The mock-up for the first batch of DLR vehicles is seen at the site of the design consultants W.S. Atkins, Epsom. The exterior view shows an early idea for the livery, with an anchor and chain link logo and orange stripes.**

Above **Inside view of the vehicle concept mock-up. The two door equipments were from different suppliers.**

New false arches built to carry the original Island Gardens platforms.

The construction of the original Canary Wharf Station into a gap in the original warehouses which were removed soon afterwards when the massive new development started. This original station was never finished.

Building the DLR

Although it may seem that the DLR was blessed with being able to use a lot of redundant railway land that no-one else had previously claimed it was still necessary to establish relations with a great number of parties before construction could begin. In particular there were more than one hundred tenants trading from arches underneath the old viaduct on the City area; at certain other places, notably south of Bow Church Station and between Mudchute and Island Gardens other very sensitive property and occupation matters had to be tackled. Two-thirds of the 7.5 route miles (12.1 km) of the 1987 opening railway uses former disused or under-used railway. Some considerable new works, in volume and variety, were necessary to accommodate the DLR.

Starting at the City end, the original terminus at Tower Gateway is constructed on a reinforced concrete viaduct. A double track viaduct, since modified and rebuilt for the Bank extension, had been constructed eastwards parallel to the BR-owned Fenchurch Street lines. In this area a reinforced concrete slab supported by the existing viaduct and independent foundations was constructed. Elsewhere an independent steel and concrete composite design has been used. At Cannon Street Road (1 km east of Tower Gateway) the DLR joined the BR viaduct and adopted two original BR running rails.

At Shadwell the BR viaduct was used to carry the island platform structure. A 200 metre reinforced concrete viaduct was constructed south of Limehouse Station (then called Stepney East) to avoid the existing BR running lines and to link into the western end of the disused brick arch viaduct of the former London & Blackwall Railway. From here to near to the north side of the West India Docks, the line used the 1839 constructed viaduct, a Grade II listed structure.

Left **Casting the track plinth south of West India Quay.**

Right **Viaduct construction at Island Gardens Platform 2.**

No fewer than 11 wrought iron bridge decks needed replacing with new concrete decks, although the old side girders were put back in to retain appearances. At West India Dock Road the two-span bridge was reconstructed to incorporate the original solid pink granite columns in the road. As originally built, the line rose up on to a standard steel and concrete composite structure leading to North Quay junction, originally built with 40-metre radius turnouts as part of three double junctions. South of this junction the Docks Crossing began. Specially fabricated 65-metre spans were provided in each of the three docks with an 8-metre clearance over the water of the dock. This structure, which in the mid-1980s dominated the skyline, soon became dwarfed by the vast office buildings around it. South of the West India Dock system, the line turns east on a 50-metre radius curve and then winds its way south through the island on standard elevated structure although a specially fabricated section was used to cross the Millwall Cut, the stretch of water connecting the West India and Millwall docks.

South of Crossharbour the line used an earth embankment before being carried on a new viaduct containing Mudchute station to join the 27 surviving arches of the single track Millwall Park viaduct. This part is now disused.

The route from North Quay junction to Poplar and Stratford was built with several one-off features. The bridge over what was the Docklands Northern Relief Road, now Aspen Way, is a 50-metre span skew plate girder bridge. Poplar Station was originally built on retained-fill immediately southwest of the Operations and Maintenance Centre. The old trackbed was re-ballasted and new drainage provided north of Poplar. A steel plate girder bridge was needed to cross the Limehouse Cut Canal south of Devons Road because the earlier structure had decayed badly.

North of Bow the Bow Curve takes the line from the old cutting to run beside British Rail on an embankment featuring a 1 in 25 gradient on a 100-metre radius curve. New ballasted track was laid towards Stratford on the alignment of the most southerly of the BR lines and only minimal engineering work was needed to adapt the western end bay platform for DLR trains to use.

The Initial Railway had been constructed under a design and build contract with GEC-Mowlem Railway Group carrying out all the tasks necessary to provide a complete railway. This formula was repeated with the extension further into the City, to Bank Station. On 17th July 1987 – before the original railway had even opened for traffic – two contracts were awarded; to Edmund Nuttall Ltd for the westward extension in tunnel to Bank, including construction of the DLR station at Bank; and to GEC-Mowlem Railway Group for the upgrading of the existing system, extension of electrical systems through the E. Nuttall contract works, and provision of new vehicles.

A single 100-tonne tunnelling machine was constructed in Britain, to a German design, to bore the tunnel part of the 1.6 km extension westwards from Royal Mint Street. Following a Start of Tunnelling ceremony on 14th March 1988 the westbound tunnel was bored first, breaking through into the new King William Street station site on 7th December 1988. The machine was then withdrawn from the westbound tunnel and put to work digging the second one, to become the eastbound tunnel. This bore was completed in February 1990. Tunnelling through the London clay was achieved at an average rate of nearly 100 metres per week.

The circular cross section tunnels were bored by the 5.39 metre diameter tunnelling machine, then lined with precast concrete segmental lining: the internal tunnel diameter is five metres. This tunnel diameter permits the provision of a walkway on one side, which allows not only access for maintenance but evacuation of passengers, including mobility-impaired passengers, in an emergency. In order to bore the seven-metre station tunnels the existing tunnelling machine was plugged into the centre of a larger 7.75 metre station tunnel machine, retaining the smaller machine's facilities to power the larger machine. As much as 200,000 tonnes of clay was excavated and taken to various sites east of London including the site of the former Beckton Gasworks. Generally, the tunnels were bored at depths greater than 30 metres below ground with the Bank Station at a depth up to 42 metres below ground.

Besides the tunnelling carried out by machine, ventilation shafts, access points, escalator shafts and interconnecting tunnels were dug by the traditional hand method. In order to minimise surface impact, available space on street corners was used for worksites: as well as the main contract site at Royal Mint Street beside the DLR, four other worksites were used at Fish Street Hill, Lombard Street, Lothbury and Bucklersbury.

Beneath the Mansion House, a Grade 1 listed building, it was necessary to dig a step-plate junction, which is a series of expanding tunnel diameters to accommodate a rail junction between the two running lines. Special tie bars were used to secure Mansion House following the necessary approvals in July 1990. The step-plate junction was completed in March 1991 and although there were some signs of movement in one corner of the building, it suffered no damage.

As well as the main work, substantial effort was needed to rebuild and integrate the London Underground station to provide links to the new DLR facilities. In particular a new concrete slab was cast above the existing station to support a new building to be constructed over the ticket hall. This required 30 metres deep hand-dug shafts to accommodate the necessary vertical piles.

At the same time as the decision-making process gave the go-ahead for the physical extension of the railway to Bank, a decision was taken to upgrade the rest of the railway to handle more passengers.

The upgrading work divided into five main parts: the strengthening of structures, where necessary, to run two-unit trains; lengthening platforms to handle these longer trains; infrastructure improvements to aid operational flexibility; buying more trains; and specific upgrading work such as the total rebuilding of Canary Wharf Station.

It may seem difficult to appreciate now, but until the advent of the Canary Wharf scheme for the Isle of Dogs it was intended that the main DLR service would be from the City to Beckton with the Isle of Dogs to be served by the north–south service from Stratford, passengers changing at Poplar between one route and the other.

One of the 'bowl' stations under construction towards the eastern end of the Beckton extension.

The main Beckton contract consisted of approximately one-third each of elevated, ground level and trough or underpass-level railway. Concrete structures which are more expensive but more substantial then the earlier steel/concrete composite design are used throughout for the elevated portions, which are located principally in the Poplar to Leamouth/Brunswick areas, at the Connaught Crossing viaduct and near Gallions Reach station.

Where the DLR crosses the River Lea a post-tensioned box girder bridge with a 74-metre span has been erected. Further east, the track descends to ground level but two stations, Beckton Park and Cyprus, were constructed in the centre of the Royal Albert Dock spine road as part of that contract. The track is also located within an underpass near the eastern end of the route in order to pass under the Eastern Gateway access road which is the main link road to the A406 North Circular Road.

Cutty Sark Station under construction, with the bored tunnels meeting the station box.

Elverson Road Station construction with the relocation of the River Ravensbourne providing space for the railway.

Resulting from the enormous creation of employment in Docklands it was soon realised that the area immediately south of the Thames needed a good connection with Canary Wharf, but the DLR could not be extended to other administrative areas using LDDC channelled finance. Lewisham borough had initially proposed the extension to Lewisham and was actively supported by Greenwich in feasibility, route and environmental studies. A Parliamentary Bill was deposited in November 1991 and received Royal Assent in May 1993.

There were to be no major problems to overcome but by virtue of the need to tunnel under the Thames and to provide a viaduct to align the project into a practical entry to Lewisham it could not be low cost. Under Government help and direction a significantly new private finance initiative was set up. This produced the full designs for a financeable scheme but showed that the cost of the river crossing would prevent a positive return to the investors. Thus private and public partnership was developed to provide the £50M difference in finance from a number of state and local sources. To enable DLR to manage the provision

of the extension it has been organised as a concession granted to a new railway and at the end of the concession all the property and assets will be transferred to DLR. This new railway attracted seven consortia to bid for the contract, and the winning group under the name City Greenwich Lewisham Rail Link PLC (CGLR) was responsible for producing the railway and will maintain the infrastructure for 25.5 years, which includes the construction phase. CGLR receives an availability fee from the opening date up to year 2009 and from then on a usage fee tied to passenger numbers. In return CGLR must make the whole extension available to year 2021 for the DLR train service operator to run the service required of it. The result has brought 500,000 more people within 45 minutes travelling time of the Docklands area. Journey times of 30 minutes from Lewisham to Bank or Stratford and 16 minutes to Canary Wharf are now on offer. Service intervals vary between 4 and 15 minutes for the different times of day and days of the week and correspond with the intervals north of the river.

The Lewisham extension joined the existing railway north of Mudchute station, with a replacement station built north of the original Mudchute stop. It then goes underground on the north side of the old Millwall Park alignment with a new sub-surface Island Gardens station constructed north of the original terminus station, which was demolished. The tunnels go under the River Thames with an underground station, called Cutty Sark, built between Thames Street and Creek Road in central Greenwich.

The line then curves south-westwards to surface near the existing Greenwich station, continuing as an elevated railway along the alignment of Deptford Creek. A station has been built at Deptford Bridge with the route then continuing principally through existing open space towards a stop at Elverson Road, proceeding to the west of Conington Road to terminate at a station south of the existing Lewisham station ticket hall.

The construction of the tunnel under the railway at Lewisham Station required the DLR structure to be jacked through the embankment supporting the railway. Railway service disruption was kept to a minimum by using this construction method.

A Stratford-bound
train passes Poplar
Depot under the
Beckton line viaduct.

The routes described

As opened in 1987 the DLR consisted of three legs meeting at a triangular junction located at the northern end of the Isle of Dogs. One leg ran westwards to the City (initially to Tower Gateway near Tower Bridge, now also to an underground station at Bank), one to Stratford to the north east and one to Island Gardens, the terminus at the southern end of the Isle of Dogs peninsular facing Greenwich and the Cutty Sark preserved sailing ship. The Beckton extension added a fourth leg to the original Poplar junction area, which has been extensively rebuilt and enlarged. The Lewisham extension extends the Isle of Dogs leg further south, and under the River Thames.

The City route

The DLR has two termini in the City of London: Bank underground station and the original elevated terminus called Tower Gateway.

Bank Station, consisting of the two side-platform tunnels bored either side of a central concourse, is located below the other existing railway tunnels at Bank. Interchange via new and existing escalators and passageways is provided to the Central, Northern, Circle, District and Waterloo & City lines of the Underground.

Eastwards from the Bank platforms, twin 5 metre diameter bored tunnels proceed and are generally underneath existing surface streets rather than buildings. The tunnels follow the alignment of King William Street towards the Monument Underground station road junction, thence under Great Tower Street, under Tower Hill between the Tower Hill ticket hall concourse of the Underground station and the Tower of London, crossing underneath Mansell Street to emerge on the north side of Royal Mint Street, climbing up above ground to join the elevated DLR structure of the original DLR Tower Gateway–Shadwell section.

The Tower Gateway terminus is built on a new structure close to the eastern end of the Fenchurch Street platforms. The DLR station is on the east side of the street called Minories, under which a public subway provides a pedestrian link to Tower Hill Underground station.

Bank Station commuters wait to join the arriving train.

Aerial view of the DLR approach to the City of London with the original terminus of Tower Gateway (centre of picture) and Fenchurch Street main line terminus beyond. The DLR cutting and tunnel mouth for the Bank line are surrounded by a car park.

From Tower Gateway the new double track structure takes the line east as far as Cannon Street Road. Between here and Stepney the DLR track moves slightly northwards on to the existing viaduct where British Rail relinquished the two most southerly of its Fenchurch Street lines. An island platform station is located at Shadwell where the east-west viaduct crosses Watney Street. The remains of the adjacent London & Blackwall station platform would have left insufficient room for the other outside platform had it been re-used. Interchange with the East London Line is provided via Watney Street and Cable Street.

Approaching Limehouse, a new structure is provided to carry the line over Butcher Row with a DLR station located east of Butcher Row allowing interchange between the Fenchurch Street line services and the DLR.

East of this station the DLR line leaves the British Rail alignment and follows the course of the London & Blackwall Railway on the 1840 built brick arch viaduct abandoned by British Railways in 1962.

It is at this point that the first signs of the contemporary Docklands area scene emerge; major construction work to the south of the DLR in the former Regents Canal dock – also called Limehouse Basin – has produced the Limehouse Link road in tunnel under Limehouse. In the middle distance can be seen the new flats near the River Thames along Narrow Street and then the spectacular Canary Wharf development rises up from the old docks on the Isle of Dogs. The line continues eastward on the former London & Blackwall brick arch viaduct crossing Westferry Road, where another station, called Westferry, is located. Then, after crossing the West India Dock Road, the dramatic and at first sight complicated junctions at North Quay are reached. Simply put, as now remodelled, there is provision for the City services to run into the junction and southwards on to the Isle of Dogs and Lewisham with the Beckton services separated away on to the Beckton Link viaduct. Trains from Stratford will continue to share the same junction north of West India Quay Station.

Shadwell Station was one of a number renewed in 1999 with a full-length glazed roof.

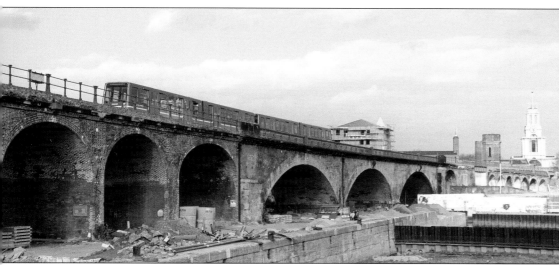

A train crosses the listed viaduct under which passes the Regents Canal at Limehouse.

Limehouse Station showing the 1999-built glazed roof now protecting the full platform lengths.

A Stratford train
curves past the
eastern end of Poplar
Depot under the
Beckton line viaduct.

The Stratford route

The line to Stratford heads east from the North Quay junction area and descends
to Poplar Station. The Operations and Maintenance Centre is on the northern side
of the railway. It is in the Poplar area that the tightest curves on the system are
to be found, at 40 metres. Leaving Poplar the line descends to ground level and
then turns northwards into a shallow cutting towards All Saints Station along a
former BR railway alignment. Alongside All Saints Station two sidings have recently
been provided for vehicle storage. Between All Saints and Devons Road Station
the line runs either slightly below ground level or at grade. Nearby features consist
of old-established council flats to the east of the line and small-scale factory units
on the western side. The line crosses the Limehouse Cut Canal at a point where
a former Spratts dog biscuit factory has been converted into residential units away
from the Thames riverside. The wooden fencing here assists in noise reduction.
East of Devons Road Station a partly-completed new industrial park has been
built on the former British Rail Devons Road motive power depot. Approaching
Bow Church Station the line runs through a rectangular concrete tunnel which
forms the base of residential units built by the Greater London Council when this
alignment was still carrying freight traffic to the docks.

All Saints Station after renewal and extension of its platform canopies in similar style to the original ones.

Poplar Depot train-washing machine is located close by Poplar High Street overbridge.

North of Bow Church the railway is reduced to a single track and a new climbing curve carries this track from the former North London Railway alignment up to the embankment of the relatively little used link between Fenchurch Street and Stratford. This latter line merges with the tracks of the Liverpool Street to Stratford multiple track alignment, with the single track DLR route simply located on the extreme south side of the embankment. This part of the route is surrounded by an industrial environment but as the train approaches Stratford there is evidence of commercial regeneration with new office blocks built near the commercial centre of Stratford. At Stratford, a bay platform never used by intended BR services to Fenchurch Street was available at the western end of Stratford's up platforms and this ultra-simple terminus arrangement is used by DLR trains. Passengers can change to main line services and London Underground's Central Line at the same level as well as to the low-level station platforms where North London Link services call and the Jubilee Line terminates.

The country branch look of the single-track curve between the alignment of the old North London Railway and that of the Great Eastern Railway at Bow.

Pudding Mill Lane Station, built to serve the industrial area along the Lea Valley. Until 1998 there was just a passing loop at this point.

Below **Stratford Terminus** has easy interchange to other services, both main line and Underground. The new station built for the Jubilee Line can be seen on the right.

The Beckton route

Like the Stratford route the Beckton extension begins at the complex of tracks
now in place at North Quay junction and serves Poplar Station using the most
northerly and southerly of the four tracks at this station; the north side track is
the Down Beckton and the south side track is the Up Beckton. The Down Beckton
flies over the Stratford tracks at the eastern end of the Operations and Maintenance
Centre and continues as an elevated railway over Preston's Road and through the
Leamouth area, an area currently still being redeveloped.

South of the alignment the remains of the former Brunswick Wharf power
station, itself built on the site of the original London and Blackwall terminus, have
been developed into another riverside housing complex. The first station on the
extension, called Blackwall, is located east of Preston's Road and the second is
East India Station south of the Aspen Way–Lower Lea Crossing road.

The line then proceeds north-eastwards around the convoluted bends of the
River Lee on its final approach to the River Thames. A significant station at
Canning Town, parallel to the A1011 Silvertown Way, is on a site that is
substantially altered to accommodate the Jubilee Line platforms, new platforms
for the North London Link service to North Woolwich and a bus station. The
Beckton line opened without Canning Town Station as the site for the new station
was not then developed.

The line to Beckton then parallels the Railtrack line southwards then eastwards into the Royal Docks area. A future stop is planned at Thames Wharf, from where the line heads east with stations called Royal Victoria, Custom House and Prince Regent, along the line which is effectively at grade here on the south side of Victoria Dock Road. A future stop is planned near the Connaught Crossing road bridge. East of this road bridge there are three further stations at Royal Albert, Beckton Park and Cyprus with the alignment running on the north side of the Royal Albert Dock and parallel to it. Along this section the line is located in the centre-line of the dual carriageway Royal Albert Dock Spine Road. The stations at Beckton Park and Cyprus are built at ground level in the centre of roundabouts with pedestrian links north and south. Footbridges take passengers under the road but over the railway: they are known as bowl stations.

After Cyprus Station the line turns northwards after first curving southwards of the large roundabout at the junction of the east–west and north–south road network at the eastern end of the Royal Docks system. The next station is at Gallions Reach immediately to the west of the alignment of the planned East London River Crossing road bridge. The Beckton depot is further to the east of Gallions Reach and will, once the road bridge is in place, be visually separated by the northern approach roads. The line then curves north westwards, to terminate at Beckton, near the existing junction of Tollgate Road and East Ham Manor Way, to the east of the existing Asda District Centre.

Prince Regent Station and the climb to Connaught Crossing in the distance.

The view eastwards on the Connaught Crossing viaduct, with the City Airport on the right beyond the Albert Dock.

The Spine road section approaching Beckton Park Station.

The access bridge between platforms and under the surrounding roadway at Cyprus Station.

Platform level view of the bowl station at Beckton Park with the road roundabout above.

A train crosses between Canary Wharf and Heron Quays, with the Jubilee Line station in the background.

The Isle of Dogs route

The route through the Isle of Dogs to Island Gardens runs from the North Quay junction area on the north side of the former West India Docks system on 1986-built bridges across all three docks of the former system. However, it is no longer easy to appreciate the fact that there are three parallel stretches of water because of the infilling of the dock for the mass of the Canary Wharf commercial, retail and leisure developments. The DLR tracks pass into the visually impressive all-over roof of Canary Wharf Station, which now has the look and scale of a major heavy rail facility.

Proceeding southwards to Heron Quays the tracks enter Heron Quays Station which remains, at the time of writing, largely in the form developed for the initial £77m railway. Heron Quays itself remains largely undeveloped but change is already beginning. It was on this quay, prior to the building of the DLR, that a Dash 7 short take-off and landing aircraft made a single landing and take-off to demonstrate the feasibility of the subsequent London City Airport.

After crossing the docks the route curves sharply to the east on a typical Light Rail style curve, and descends slightly to the station at South Quay before rising again to cross the Millwall Cut, the narrow section of water linking the former West India Dock System with the Millwall Docks. From here the line continues, still on newly-built viaduct, towards Crossharbour Station. Between South Quay and Crossharbour the line curves to the south apparently following the shape of the Harbour Exchange office development, but in fact the railway was erected first, and the offices were designed to follow the DLR alignment. Crossharbour Station is located on the south-east side of the London Arena and to the north-west of the Asda store which serves as a district centre.

The grand overall roof of Canary Wharf sits between the high-rise developments.

South Quay Station as rebuilt after bomb damage.

The view from Crossharbour Station with the London Arena, which generates huge off-peak traffic for the railway.

After Crossharbour the original DLR route followed the alignment of a disused railway embankment carrying the line south beside East Ferry Road to a point where it turned east and crossed the road on a new section of bridge structure which also supported Mudchute Station. South of Mudchute the route rejoined the 1872 built single-track viaduct which ran through the south western corner of Millwall Park, reaching Manchester Road. A new bridge section carried the line across Manchester Road to a simple 'V' plan layout terminus with two linked side platforms at Island Gardens. All the DLR infrastructure south of Crossharbour was removed during 1999 during construction of the Lewisham Extension and new stations were built at Mudchute and Island Gardens.

The route continues from Mudchute into a cut and cover tunnel with a gentle down grade to Island Gardens which is a central island in a below-ground box and partially roofed over. The cut and cover tunnel is arranged as two single track covered ways. Immediately after Island Gardens the under river bored tunnel starts and has a gradient of up to 6% each side of the centre river sump. The station at Cutty Sark is in a cut and cover box and has a central island platform. Because of the depth of Cutty Sark Station the first part of the section on to Greenwich also has to be in bored tunnel. This section of tunnel ends for each bore in a chamber from which the boring machine was dismantled and removed. Beyond these chambers the form of construction reverts to cut and cover.

The centre island platform for the new Island Gardens Station, showing clean and simple structures.

Cutty Sark Station lower escalator passing through the mezzanine floor where the substation is located.

In order to fit in a DLR station at Greenwich adjacent to the National Railways facility, considerable rearrangement of existing facilities took place. The resultant DLR location has required the cut and cover tunnel to continue south and west under the National Railway lines and under the Greenwich Station platform and rise to a DLR station at the western end of the site. Thus DLR now sits on the track location of the original London and Greenwich Railway terminal tracks. The continuation of the extension now takes it along and over the course of the lowest reach of the River Ravensbourne which is tidal and known as Deptford Creek. A 20 span 800m long post-tensioned concrete viaduct takes a twisting path to Deptford Bridge Station. The next section sees the line return to ground level and fit into the river valley beside the Ravensbourne. The whole section has been created by realigning the river along to Elverson Road Station in conjunction with parkland and flood protection works. Special care was involved as this area also has part of the chalk aquapha coming to the surface and drinking water contamination had to be protected against. Elverson Road Station is approached via a reverse curve and the route continues on the short distance to Lewisham Station.

A view approaching Greenwich from Lewisham with Connex lines sharing a joint station.

Facing page **Deptford Bridge Station** located over the busy A2 road shows the viaduct fitted snugly between the buildings of Lewisham College and over the River Ravensbourne.

Left **Elverson Road Station** serves a well-populated residential area to the north of Lewisham centre.

Left **Lewisham Station** showing the new DLR facility and the new bus station, both located between the two railway routes the station serves.

DLR trains

On any railway, the trains present the most important element of a passenger's journey. It is now generally recognised that a train is not solely a functional piece of hardware, but an essential part of the image, both in external appearance and the internal finish and comfort. This was realised by the railways' joint clients and by the contractor, and substantial efforts were made to ensure high standards of engineering and finish.

In the context of the DLR in its initial form, evolving a whole new design for just 11 vehicles could not be justified. Main contractor GEC-Mowlem therefore co-operated with Linke Hofmann Busch (LHB), one of Germany's main builders of light railway vehicles. The eleven vehicles of what became known as 'P86' stock, were delivered by road and sea via Hamburg and King's Lynn from August 1986, the first (01) arriving at Poplar on 7th August 1986. The last vehicle of the first batch, No. 11, was to make history several times. It was delivered direct to Debdale Park, Manchester on 9th February 1987 as the key part of a light rail demonstration where it became the first revenue-earning DLR vehicle. The vehicle was temporarily modified to accept a pantograph for the overhead power collection system installed by Balfour Beatty, a conversion which was remarkably simple involving little more that an additional roof member and a length of conduit to carry the main power cables down to its underframe. Vehicle 11 was thus the last to be delivered to the DLR at Poplar on 30th March 1987. In the hands of Train Captain Gary Bonini, No. 11 carried Her Majesty the Queen and His Royal Highness the Duke of Edinburgh from Island Gardens to Poplar, and thence to Tower Gateway, on the occasion of the Royal Opening of the railway on 30th July 1987. Vehicle 11 was also the first to be despatched to its new owners in Essen, Germany, on 14th November 1991.

There were 84 seats in each car, mostly arranged in transverse bays of four to take full advantage of the large windows offering fine rooftop views of the changing Docklands scene. Nowhere is this more true than in the end seats, giving front seat passengers an almost unprecedented driver's eye view. An emergency driving console for the Train Captain was provided in the centre of the screen, locked when not in use. To increase circulation space, 12 longitudinal seats were provided in the centre section of the train, along with two wheelchair bays. The railway has some regular wheelchair users, but the bays are most heavily used by shoppers with wheeled trolleys and baby buggies, taking advantage of the railway's superb roll-on/roll-off facilities. In order to achieve good access for unassisted wheelchair users, the cars were designed to have a level car floor to platform gap of only 75mm (about 3 inches). This led to the adoption of inward-opening ('bat wing') swing plug doors. These were never an ideal solution but, with the traffic levels forecast at the time the contract was awarded, it was anticipated that the layout would be acceptable.

The initial fleet of eleven vehicles was supplemented by a further ten – the P89 stock – to increase the capacity of the Initial Railway and for the first phase of services underground to Bank. These vehicles were very similar to the first (P86) batch with only detailed modifications – mostly under the skin – made in the light of operational experience, the need for longer (two-vehicle) trains, and to enable them to operate underground to Bank. P86 cars were prohibited from underground running, as they did not meet tunnel running safety requirements.

The additional ten vehicles were ordered as part of the upgrading contract in July 1987 and differed from the initial vehicles in that they were constructed in the UK. During 1986 BREL decided to enter the light rail market and entered a co-operative agreement with LHB, whose products are largely complementary to those of the UK builder. The DLR vehicles were the first products of this development, being sub-contracted by GEC-Mowlem Railway Group to BREL, York. Numbered in the series 12-21, the first vehicle (No. 12) was delivered by road, arriving at Poplar on 12th December 1989, the last one (No. 21) on 4th May 1990. After commissioning and trials, the first to enter service (No. 12) did so on 11th May 1990.

The only cosmetic difference between the P89 vehicles as built and the first batch was in the destination displays. On the newer vehicles these were in the form of 'Voltron' illuminated displays, which were far more reliable than the original equipment on the P86 cars. On the older vehicles, many had succumbed to having hand-operated swivelling destination boxes but in May 1990 unit 01 was fitted with 'Voltron' destination displays and the whole P86 fleet was subsequently so converted. Other changed features included the fitting of bulbous panels by the (inward) opening doors to both the P86 and P89 trains, in an attempt to discourage passengers from standing in that area, and blue-tinted fluorescent lights at the 'driving' ends to reduce reflection for Train Captains when driving manually in the darkened conditions. From 15th June 1991, trains appeared in service with London Transport 'Light Rail' roundels applied to the front ends and the centre sides of each section. These were removed when responsibility for the DLR was transferred to the LDDC.

A train captain operating the train in automatic mode but using the door controls at the emergency driving position. This can be done to allow the train captain to observe from the front without driving manually when station equipment has failed.

Interior of B stock showing the articulation area with equipment cupboard to the left of the turntable.

It was originally envisaged that the P89 stock would be sufficient for the Bank extension, but the unprecedented increases in passenger traffic and the authorised extension to Beckton highlighted the need for even more trains, and the capability to operate double length (two-vehicle) trains wherever possible. A contract was subsequently awarded to BN Constructions Ferrovaires et Metalliques of Bruges in Belgium, initially for ten more vehicles of what became known as the B90 stock. This would have given a total of 31 vehicles in the DLR fleet (11×P86, 10×P89 and 10×B90), but the BN order was increased to 21 vehicles (11×P86, 10×P89 and 21×B90 – total 42). A mock-up of the new BN stock was made available for public inspection in late September/early October 1989, by which time the requirement for additional stock from BN had grown to 44 vehicles (11×P86, 10×P89 and 44×B90 – total 65).

Perhaps the most noticeable feature of the B stock is its sliding doors, provided to improve boarding and alighting at stations, necessary because of the far greater usage of the DLR than was originally envisaged. These doors, outside-mounted, form part of the loading gauge and the width of the main vehicle body is thus fractionally less than the P stock. Other different features include fewer transverse seats (allowing a greater standing capacity within the train), a front opening door allowing access between coupled units (superfluous apart from in emergency situations, since there are no footplates over the couplers between units, and in the tunnels in an emergency, access and detrainment is via the side doors onto specially provided side tunnel platform walkways). The front seats for forward viewing remain, however, although the emergency driving console for the Train Captain has had to be 'split' into two sections, one on each side of the front door. The door operating panel for the Train Captain is located down the left hand side of the double doorway positions, rather than over the doorways as on the P stock and conventionally upholstered seats replace inset moquette panels used hitherto. All of the electronic equipment is located in a two locked interior cabinet, rather than in several different positions.

B92 vehicle door vestibule showing the train captain's control panel on the left side and passenger alarm on the right side.

B92 vehicle showing the outside-hung sliding door in closed position.

Doors in open position showing centre grab pole. The door panels are used for advertising promotions.

The final order for B stock comprised 70 vehicles, divided into two sub-types – 23 units of B90 stock (numbered 22–44) and 47 units of B92 stock (45–91). The first vehicle of B90 stock arrived via Dartford Docks at Poplar on 31st January 1991 and was available for test running and crew training from 23rd April. The last unit arrived on 27th September. The first to enter service (vehicle 22) did so on 1st July 1991. These trains, like the P89 stock, are able to operate singly or two coupled together, but the two types were not compatible. Four trains (22, 24–26) were delivered with continental style vehicle numbers, but the rest were delivered with numbers in the New Johnston style as used by London Transport – the first four were later altered to be identical. 'Light Rail' roundels were to be fitted to the B90 vehicles, but only 14 B90 vehicles received them. The others were not given roundels due to the impending announcement that the DLR was to be taken over by the London Docklands Development Corporation, which happened from 1st April 1992. All but three B90 vehicles were in service by November 1991, except for 23 and 25 (which were test trains – both were in service by the summer of 1992) and the B92 prototype, unit 35. This was fitted from the start with Alcatel equipment for testing purposes – a section of Beckton extension track in the Poplar area was set aside for trial and test running from 9th September 1991. Joining vehicle 35, the first two Alcatel-equipped B92 vehicles proper arrived at Poplar in October 1991, to give three units for testing. All of the other B92 vehicles were delivered direct to Beckton depot, equipped from the start with Alcatel equipment. The first of these arrived on 10th March 1992 and testing began soon after between Prince Regent and Beckton. The first vehicle to be delivered was 58 – not the first in the series. Vehicles 47–57 followed later because of equipment shortages at the construction stage.

Deliveries of the B92 stock continued throughout 1992 and into 1993, the last (91) arriving on 15th March 1993. The first vehicle to operate under its own power between Poplar and Beckton throughout was vehicle 86 on 10th November 1992. Commissioning of the signalling and the point work in Beckton depot resulted in 21 vehicles being outstabled from 16th June 1993 at Canning Town. They were moved one week later to the East India viaduct, out of the way of hooligans and graffiti vandals, where they remained until 18th July 1993.

The B90 stock, although equipped for operating the original GEC signalling system, was easily converted to Alcatel in readiness for system-wide operation. To that end, the first vehicle (22) was withdrawn for conversion on 29th October 1993, re-entering service with its B92 counterparts on the Beckton branch open day, 28th March 1994. Three other vehicles (23, 24 and 42) were withdrawn for conversion before the old signalling system was taken out of use on 7th July 1995, but the remaining B90 vehicles continued in service on the other routes until that date. Conversion of these then followed, the last being vehicle 28 completed in April 1998.

Following the derailment of No. 45 between West India Quay and Canary Wharf on 21st October 1995 it returned to service on 6th November 1995 in an experimental 'Corporate' livery of petrol blue and silver. This actually comprised adhesive vinyl over the old colours. In this, it remained unique until given a polyester all-over-advert livery in November 1998.

Interior of a B92 vehicle as delivered. Each has a total capacity of 284 passengers, including 70 seated.

Crucial to the efficient operation of the railway is adherence to the laid down station dwell times, which can be made more difficult by increasing numbers of passengers. A number of trials were thus made to speed up passenger movement on the B90 stock. These included placing the opening of the train doors under the control of the Train Captain (July to November 1992) and different applications of the door-close signal. The method adopted saw the door-close bleep sound as the doors close, rather than before, which was in fact standardising a feature already on the B92 trains, a modification which was completed in May 1995. This has resulted in a highly reliable railway, achieved through disciplined Train Captains ensuring a prompt departure from stations.

The 11 vehicles of P86 stock were purchased by Essener Verkehrs AG of Essen in 1991 for further service and with their new owners were fitted with pantographs and cabs. The vehicles were renumbered from 01-11 to 5201-5211 respectively, the first to enter service on the Essen U-Bahn system being 06 and 11 in November 1994. Conversion of the remaining vehicles was completed by early-1999.

Although the P89 stock, converted to sliding doors in 1991/92, was able to operate over the whole of the Initial Railway, including the underground section to Bank, extensive upgrading work would have been required for it to work on the Alcatel system. All ten vehicles were thus withdrawn on 7 July 1995, the last day of the GEC signalling system, and over that weekend were transferred to Beckton for storage. The decision was later taken to sell these ten vehicles to Essen as well as the P86s, but not before a trial Alcatel conversion had been undertaken on vehicle 13 in April 1996. Between 12th December 1996 and 8th August 1997, the ten (12-21) were gradually transferred to Essen. They have been renumbered 5221-5230 respectively, and the first conversion to Essen standards entered service in the summer of 1999 in yellow livery.

Because of the ever-increasing numbers of passengers using the DLR, especially the Bank branch in the peaks, measures for increased vehicle capacity were undertaken. The result was an internal rearrangement of vehicle 32, where additional standing space was created, but at the expense of 20 seats throughout the vehicle, or ten per centre bay. Grab rails replaced grab handles and much extra standing room was available in the door area. Whilst successful in its way, a modified design which enabled greater standing room was subsequently agreed upon, with a total of 20 vehicles to be so converted. The first to be completed was 50 on 21st December 1998. The other 19 followed and comprised 51-67, along with 45 and 32. The last two took the place of 68 and 69, because of advertising requirements (45) and the need to standardise the prototype (32), the latter being the last to be converted in April 1999. Wherever possible, it is endeavoured to have at least one of these maximum capacity units on each Bank train in the peaks.

Advertising is always a useful source of additional income and from mid-February 1996 adverts for BCM (Bell Cablemedia) were applied to exterior train doors below the windows. Other advertisers have since taken advantage, including the occasion of the 10th anniversary of the Docklands Light Railway, when some vehicles were sponsored for 'Save the Children' fund. The first all-over advert vehicle was applied to vehicle 74 in October 1998, a local venture for the London

To cope with increased demand, partly caused by delays to the opening of the Jubilee Line extension, twenty vehicles for the Bank service were converted to a revised interior layout in 1998 and 1999. These gave more standing space by changing some of the transverse seats for longitudinal ones and setting them back from the door areas. More handrails were installed as part of the work, which reduced the seating capacity from 70 to 50 per vehicle.

The original interior layout is retained on 50 vehicles as shown here in one of the later built group.

Knights Ice Hockey Team, followed by another, but not quite identical advert, on 45 on November 1998. The latter saw the end of the prototype petrol blue corporate livery. Compaq computers then sponsored four vehicles in a mainly white livery – 48–51 – from mid-April 1999, and these were followed by an all-over advert for Jaguar cars on 67 and 68 from the end of June 1999. Nos 46 and 47 were sponsored by Lewisham Shopping Centre from early November 1999 ready for the extension to open. Although the remainder of the fleet still looks smart in its original red and blue livery, the Docklands Light Railway are anticipating that other organisations will use their trains for advertising in the future.

In October 1999 DLR were given permission from the Department of Transport, Environment and the Regions to start the process of purchasing 12 new vehicles. Those reading this handbook will have appreciated that DLR and thus its existing vehicles are very much an integrated system. Thus a large amount of the specification of the new vehicles has to be along the lines of 'more of the same'. There has to be total compatibility between this new group of vehicles and the older ones. They are to be considered the same type both for the passenger environment and technical integration needs. DLR has negotiated to allow Bombardier Eurorail based in Brugge, Belgium to build these vehicles as that company supplied the present fleet. DLR will own the new fleet and they will be operated by the franchise holder. The present franchise operator DRML will ensure the integration is complete and manage any equipment changes that have to be accepted so that safety and operation are identical with the existing fleet.

The first all-over advertising to be carried by a DLR train was for the local London Knights Ice Hockey team.

A train of Compaq computer advertising vehicles at Island Gardens on opening day.

The Jaguar train of units 67 and 68 approaches Heron Quays from Canary Wharf.

The Lewisham Shopping Centre train is seen at Crossharbour.

A night view of one of the more recent stations, Mudchute, which replaced the original station here in 1999.

Station design

Even though the original plans for the railway were based around using Light Rail technology, little of the ultra-simplicity of typical European Light Rail was incorporated into DLR station design.

Whereas low platforms (with or without ramp access to trains) and bus type shelters are typical of even new systems, the DLR design consultants evolved by 1984 a more sophisticated package incorporating high level traditional British platforms, lifts and lift towers and high arched platform canopies. The design of the stops also inevitably grew visually once the elevated route had been adopted, particularly where all-new construction was envisaged on the Isle of Dogs; it was helpful to the image to have the station structures on view.

However, in one important respect the stations remained simple and cheap to operate and that was in the decision to leave them unstaffed, security relying instead on closed-circuit television, spot-checks and a frequent train service. This policy led to considerable local apprehension, expressed by residents' groups and the Docklands Forum, an active pressure group. However, not only have the stations remained remarkably safe for passengers but the incidence of graffiti and vandalism has not been the curse it was predicted to be.

However, the elevated location of most of the original stations has been a cause of justifiable complaint when passengers have been exposed to strong winds blowing across the expanses of nearby water. The balance of facilities was probably about right in relation to the proposed frequency of service and budget of the original railway and most of the original stations have been provided with better shelter since opening.

The initial railway had to be constructed to a strict and frugal budget which was achieved using a virtually standard kit of parts from which most stations could be provided. All stations required platforms raised up 1000mm above rail head so that the vehicle floor nominally maintained at 1025mm is only slightly above the platform. All platforms were initially provided with a canopy area less than the full length of the platform, a semicircular arch continuously glazed with polycarbonate panels. With a semicircular shape a high degree of self cleaning is achieved. This arch was light and airy but provided good cover for waiting passengers. It was generally arranged to be adjacent to the entrance steps and these were positioned according to the restrictions of each site. All the platform train indicator and public address equipment was fixed in the canopy. Since the back and end walls surrounding most platforms were provided from a kit assembly of panels that had fixing places on the top of each upright it was easy to fix a canopy or lighting columns as needed along the platform. For the original railway most stations have side platforms but the original Poplar had centre islands forming four platform faces, with both Tower Gateway and Shadwell having a single centre island. These island platforms required the arch roof canopy to be mounted on central columns. An original station completely different from the others is Stratford because it used an already existing but unused platform of the existing much bigger station. The standard DLR equipment had to be fitted around the existing canopy supports and the ticket machine was included in the wall of the equipment room to keep all the facilities together and preserve the one platform solely for DLR. Some additional canopy provision was made later since the expansion to two vehicle trains forced many passengers to endure poor weather without any protection for a time.

As role model for the original railway, Heron Quays remains largely unaltered except for the lenghening of its platforms carried out as part of the upgrading works. Its future is closely connected to development plans for the area.

The original City terminus at Tower Gateway is unlike any of the other stations. L-shaped in plan and elevated, its original entrance is approached via a glass rotunda at the foot of the DLR's original two escalators (plus a stairway). A second exit at the eastern end of the island platform was opened in 1990 and an additional staircase added at the west end alongside the original ones.

Almost as soon as the railway opened in 1987 the work to extend stations had to start, and for the simple side platform arrangement this was easy to achieve. It did mean a few equipment rooms needed to be moved and the track crossover at Bow Church had to be moved southwards. On the extended platforms the CCTV cameras were often the only thing moved. The real difference will always be from the original but never opened Canary Wharf to the huge and dramatic complex that serves the centre of commerce now built around the old dock wharfs.

The only new station provided along with the upgrading of the original stations was at Bank. This bored tunnel station being at rail level 42 metres below street was designed to be the new major connection of DLR into the City of London and since the Bank Station complex was already a major transport hub the DLR was slotted in as another layer below all the others. DLR facilities at platform level are the same as elsewhere and a control room is provided to manage passengers' needs. No ticketing facilities are provided for DLR as these are part of the Underground provision. The station is owned by London Underground but the tunnels are owned by DLR.

As first built Canary Wharf Station was based on the Heron Quays model but was dismantled and replaced by the present design incorporating two island platforms and two side platforms. Its distinctive overall roof and escalator provision give it a definite 'big railway' image.

South Quay was similar to Heron Quays as originally built. The extension to double length resulted in slightly offset platforms. The very heavy usage of this station has required extensive rebuilding of stairways on safety grounds. Full length platform canopies have also been provided. This work started in January 1994 and the station remained open throughout. The station had to be rebuilt again as the result of IRA bomb damage.

West India Quay after rebuilding to four tracks produced a station different from others in terms of its roof design.

Towards the end of the 1990s many of the original stations received considerable improvement in the passenger environment. Various extensions to, or complete replacements of, canopy roofs have been carried out. The more heavily used west leg and south leg stations with side platforms have been fitted with an overall roof, glazed over both platforms but not in the centre over the track. The island platforms at Shadwell and Tower Gateway have a new grander version of the original canopy which extends the full platform length. The north leg intermediate stations have lower traffic levels and the canopy improvements installed have been based on extending the existing design, using new units, to provide cover along the whole of the platform.

Left **Bow Church** Station now has a full length roof and its stairway to street level has a glazed roof.

Below **All Saints** Station shows the roof to platform 2 on the left and the new stairway cover on the right. The square section bar just below the cover is the automatic passenger counter.

The need for a second generation of stations resulted from the Beckton Extension and its place in the regeneration of the Royal Docks area. The original railway had grown in provision of station capacity as the traffic produced from the huge developments of the older docks swarmed onto the platforms. The extensions had to be tailored into the old with a less than integrated visual result; anything else would have needed closing sections for more drastic change. With the Beckton Extension the opportunity arrived to provide a newer design to fulfil the capacity need now perceived for the stations and also get a track layout where the Beckton line connected into the older lines which gave the operator the flexibility required. The completely new flying junctions west of Poplar allowed Poplar to be provided with four platforms, thus forcing the complete rebuilding of track and station. On opening on 28th March 1994 the Beckton line was a shuttle and operated separately, but from July 1995 with the conversion of the whole railway to Alcatal signalling the Beckton extension became integrated as the East leg of DLR.

The station facilities are the same as for the upgraded original stations but the station architecture is very different. The canopies are not an arch but more like a gull wing when viewed along their length and cover about half the two-vehicle length of each platform. The canopy is completely glazed in flat glass sheets. The support structure consists of round columns from which alarm boxes and signage are mounted. The platform train indicators, loudspeakers and lighting are suspended from the glazing bars to give the impression of openness in design. The original light fitting design proved very difficult to maintain and has been replaced with functional and simple industrial units giving also higher light levels to the platform area. The general colour scheme is also the petrol blue and silver chosen for the DLR when it was transferred to the London Docklands Development Corporation (LDDC). There is minimal difference in layout between side or island platforms. All platform surrounds and access ways are fitted with fully glazed panels for complete feeling of light and openness. This also gives no hiding place for troublemakers, thus giving passengers perception of lower risk to themselves. The lift towers are also much more prominent in that they have illuminated panels on top in red colour to act as a more visible sign for the station.

As before all platforms have mobility impaired access which is provided by lifts except at Beckton where the platform to street difference can be overcome with a ramp. East India has extra escalators to cater for throughput of the adjacent office complex and this is still achieved within the same architecture.

With the opening of interchange with the Jubilee Line a massive three railway station complex is in service at Canning Town and is operated by the Underground. Again the services provided for DLR are the same as everywhere else but the scale of the site including the new bus station has dramatically improved public transport provision in this area. The next big change on the way to completion is the ExCel Exhibition complex fast rising from the dockside dereliction at Custom House. The scale of capacity needed for the connection into the site has resulted in the station needing to be upgraded with a new bridge.

As built, Poplar Station featured three tracks serving two island platforms and two lifts. Rebuilding was carried out in connection with the extension of the DLR to Beckton to provide a four-track, two island platform layout. An overhead bridge links the platforms to both Poplar High Street and Aspen Way. The bridge provides a good view of the viaduct between West India Quay and Poplar stations.

Night-time scene of Poplar Station taken from the tubular overbridge, with a Stratford-bound train in view.

East India is unusual in that it is on three levels with the concourse at mezzanine level and platforms at high level. A footbridge across the adjacent dual carriageway links a major development to the north directly into the concourse, and escalators are provided from here to the two side platforms. Provision has been made for another major development to the south of the station. In other respects it is typical of Beckton line architecture.

Prince Regent Station is at the beginning of the Connaught Viaduct and is slightly elevated. The adjacent development site gives the probability of high peak passenger flows, and the single island platform here and staircases are wider than normal. A wide high level walkway links the station with a bus station on Victoria Dock Road and provides for London City Airport.

Beckton Park and Cyprus are of identical design. In this area the DLR runs in the centre reserve of the Royal Albert Dock Spine Road and these two stations are built under elevated roundabouts. Entrance to the stations is from adjacent residential streets, underneath the roundabout. A footbridge provides access to the other side of the DLR with a short staircase and ramps leading down to the two platforms.

Beckton is a simple centre platform terminus station with a short staircase and ramp leading down from the end of the platform to the adjacent street. Ticket machines and staff amenities are on the platform.

The DLR platform at Canning Town is situated immediately above the Jubilee Line station and adjacent to the Silverlink line and a bus station, forming a major interchange brought into service in 1999.

The extension to Lewisham was achieved as a project controlled and specified under the needs of financial return on investment for the concession holder City Greenwich and Lewisham Railway (CGLR). The open-air stations fall into the same design needs as the majority of stations built earlier. Those stations underground are more in common with that at Bank, except that they are box-section cut and cover rather than tube.

The main difference at above ground stations is in the design of the canopies. For lower maintenance there are only short canopy sections and these have metal panelled roofs rather than glazed ones. Each platform has two separate sections of canopy.

Both underground stations have an island platform and although the basic equipment is the same the individual design is very different. Island Gardens, being close to the surface, has the southern part open to the sky and access is by stairs. Cutty Sark is 20 metres below the surface at track level and has two mezzanine levels and escalators. Lifts for the mobility impaired are provided at both, in common with the rest of the system.

The site design at Cutty Sark provides for commercial development from ground floor upwards; thus the ticket machines and station entrance are temporarily positioned. As at Bank, both Cutty Sark and Island Gardens must have a minimum of two staff on duty when open for service.

The terminus at Lewisham is semi-underground as the site is not flat. There is a staircase at one end and same level interchange out to the adjacent bus station at the other end.

Above left **Close-up view of the canopy and seating provision on the open-air stations on the Lewisham extension.**

Above **A train from Lewisham emerges from the tube tunnelling into the cut and cover Island Gardens Station.**

Left **Cutty Sark Station upper mezzanine floor with the tunnel boring machine faceplate set into the wall to show passengers how the tunnels were dug.**

Above **The new street level building at Island Gardens cleverly integrates the tunnel ventilation towers into its design.**

Right **Cutty Sark Station platforms provide a good view of the tunnelling. The pale blue panelling is used extensively here and at Island Gardens.**

Lewisham Station has three entrances: the main one onto the street (shown below); stairs midway along the platform connecting with the bus station; and another set of stairs to the railway station.

Fares and tickets

The DLR fare structure follows the London zonal fare system beginning in Zone 1 at Bank and Tower Gateway, through Zone 2 for the majority of its stations to Stratford which is in Zone 3. The Beckton line extends to Zone 3 also and stations south of the Thames are each in both Zones 2 and 3. Initially a method of using locally purchased tickets varied from the London norm by requiring a two-step approach: first the purchase of a ticket from multi-destination machines and then its single validation in a separate validator immediately before travelling on the railway.

Although the DLR sought to establish a strong local identity this has, to an extent, clashed with passengers' awareness of the acceptance of standard Travelcards issued at other railway stations as such tickets do not require validation in DLR station validators. This was initially a cause of some confusion to passengers. In every case, passengers entering DLR stations and crossing the red line painted at station thresholds are required to have a valid ticket.

Earlier 1986-era plans to sell DLR tickets in multiple in packets at such outlets as Building Society premises for later validation were not proceeded with. Currently DLR machine-issued tickets are compatible with London Underground's ticketing system for journeys through to London Underground stations and are also valid to certain British Rail destinations in Essex. A 'Docklander' ticket is available giving unlimited travel for one day on the DLR.

The original ticket equipment consisted of Tollpoint ticket machines and Travelog ticket validators supplied by Thorn-EMI Electronics, Wells, Somerset. Unlike certain Swiss/German validators the DLR type did not cut off any part of the DLR ticket to validate it; rather tickets were absorbed completely into the validator, read and returned in seconds to the traveller. Given that no other remote ticket outlets were selling DLR type tickets, it was found possible and desirable to dispense with separate validation completely. Ticket machines were converted to issue ready-validated tickets at Tower Gateway on 5th June 1989 and elsewhere on the railway seven days later. New Westinghouse machines installed in 1991 at Tower Gateway and Canary Wharf took £5 and £10 notes. These were also installed on all the Beckton Extension stations.

As part of the improvements to the whole railway, DLR chose to replace all the ticket machines on the railway with the same new machines from Schlumberger Industries Ltd of France installed for Lewisham. These new machines greatly extend the range of tickets available and forms of payment accepted. The infrared automatic passenger counting system supplied by Acorel in France which was commissioned on the railway in 1997 has been extended to cover the Lewisham line. This system provides accurate passenger numbers to ensure the railway can justify getting its proper share of Travelcard scheme revenues.

The only change in fare zones was introduced on 9th January 2000 when the section from Beckton Park to Beckton was changed from Zone 4 to Zone 3 to encourage travel.

A standard single ticket and a Docklander, giving a day's unlimited travel on DLR.

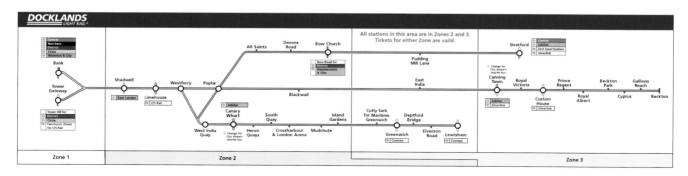

Railway headquarters and offices

Planned as a local operation, the DLR developed with its own physically separate headquarters and train depot, referred to as the Operations and Maintenance Centre. The OMC came into use at the beginning of 1987 and has since been extended in a number of ways to try to accommodate the growing business. (Located in Poplar, on former railway land south of Poplar High Street, the original OMC consists of a steel framed building on piled foundations with offices at the western end and a three track workshop to the east.) The original stabling sidings on the north side of this structure have been twice increased in number, initially close to the OMC but more recently on spare land parallel to the running lines south of All Saints. New office structures have been built on the other side of the OMC site and the rebuilding of Poplar Station and the Beckton route flyover alignments have further impacted on what has become a fully utilised busy base.

The opportunity was taken with the Beckton extension to create a new depot site at the extreme eastern end of the line to the east of Gallions Reach Station and to the east of the alignment of the future East London River Crossing (ELRC) bridge approach road. This new facility is needed to house and maintain a significant part of the increased fleet. The original concept of the initial railway of 11 vehicles using extensive offsite contractors' maintenance facilities is no longer appropriate. Beckton depot is equipped to a standard appropriate for 70–80 vehicles allowing space for efficient working on maintenance.

The OMC site at Poplar remains both as a central administration base and an operating base needed for flexibility of working. The stabling of trains will continue as will light maintenance. Both the train operating depots have full signalling and these are run from their own dedicated control room console. Poplar control room also now incorporates much improved facilities to regulate the working of train captains.

The original concepts of the small control room run essentially by one person have long been proved inadequate to operate the railway. The upgrading and extension work was always behind the passenger flows being demanded and this situation led to the decisions being made to resignal the railway with the intent of improving the throughput of trains. The many other changes to subsidiary systems such major works entail resulted in the best long term solution being a New Control Centre (NCC).

The NCC has been built at Poplar within the site boundary of the OMC. It houses all the systems needed to run the passenger railway and provides a substantially increased size of control room. The control room has space provision for the levels of staff needed and directly adjacent manager's office and personal needs facilities. The new signalling system is controlled from here and the operation has been built up during the testing and commissioning of the Beckton extension. All operation is from the NCC.

Inside view of Beckton Depot showing the maintenance pit allowing full access to equipment underneath. Access inside is by the moveable stairways in the centre of the picture.

Signalling

The first premise of the Initial Railway signalling and train control was that all the equipment must have been in use on other railways before the designs could be accepted by DLR. Thus the successful contracting group GEC-Mowlem installed a signalling system drawing heavily on the already established British Rail Solid State Interlocking (SSI). Instead of visible signals on the lineside the use of systems of track-to-train tone transmission allowed each train to be controlled safely and manually driven safely. The system of fixed block signalling was the basis of keeping trains a safe distance apart. The use of train carried micro-computers meant that the speed/distance running information could be stored on each vehicle's ATO system. This was largely adequate for the Initial Railway with its small fleet of trains.

The upgrading of the railway needed more of the same by reducing block length and installing more equipment at the trackside and on more trains. The extension of service to 2-unit trains was designed to allow single-unit trains the flexibility of continuing to stop nearest the platform entry/exit place. This immensely complicated the ATO needs but the P89 trains achieved it after midnight oil was burnt by contractors' engineers. Later the same lessons were learnt by the different ATO contractor for the B90 vehicles and they too became reliable.

On top of all this equipment of track and trains a system of Automatic Train Supervision (ATS) was produced to automate as much as possible the service running of trains and display information to operators in the control room at the OMC. As the railway settled down and services were varied to meet significantly rising demand, the restrictions of fixed block working and a system which was essentially unidirectional began to be realised. For the Beckton extension an opportunity was presented to re-think and see if a financial case was available to change to something with higher flexibility.

Late in 1989 and in early 1990 a performance specification was assembled for contractors to bid to for full resignalling of DLR. The specification allowed any proven system to be supplied but still retained the basic premise that no significantly new systems would be considered.

At the conclusion of bidding two companies survived to be fully evaluated. One offered a system based on traditional fixed block with many additions. The other was offering the concept of moving block which was already in service in Canada and potentially offered higher capacity of working.

Thus in May 1990 the Alcatel company from its Canadian SEL division received a contract to resignal the railway and had the benefit of providing the original equipment of the Beckton branch as a test track.

The basis of the resignalling scheme is a system of moving block with full bi-directional working on all tracks. This centres on the system called SELTRAC and consists of a central control system continuously communicating with all vehicles within the control area. The control area is divided up into sections each approximately 6.25m long and the trains can be followed by the central control to this level of accuracy. The system takes account of the circumstances surrounding each train and instructs each train what it should do. As a result the trains can run closer together and the capacity of the railway is thereby increased.

The operational modes of the trains have been designed to carry on the original system's flexibility with both automatic and manually driven modes controlled and protected by SELTRAC as well as the restricted emergency shunt mode for depot running or mainline recovery from failure. With SELTRAC any vehicle in a train can be in control, which will provide DLR with much needed improved reliability of public service with two-vehicle trains.

The system design caters for three-vehicle trains should this ever be considered in the future.

The principal mechanism used as a back up for SELTRAC is a system of fixed block train tracking using axle counters. This enables trains to be followed and points locked without the use of any track circuits. This allows for a much simpler arrangement of connections to the rails and easy installation on the original railway. As a back-up system DLR are able to move trains at low speed to keep passengers moving on their journeys.

Following the opening of the Beckton line and the conversion of the rest of the railway to the Alcatel Signalling System it has been necessary to make considerable improvements. Whilst the major motivator for change has been the extension to Lewisham there will always be the need to keep ahead of the needs of maintenance with modern technology. The Alcatel moving block system was installed using the mini-computer systems on which the software was run to control all the trains. This equipment design dated back to the late 1970s and was becoming difficult to keep working. It has become an unfortunate fact of life that the development and safety proving part of signalling with computers is often longer than the life span of the hardware needed, so by 1996 is was clear that there had to be a catching up contract to ensure the new system could be maintained.

Thus the move was begun to take out the original physically large but limited power old mini-computers and change to running the railway on desk top machines. The conversion of the system in Vancouver provided the example on which to build confidence in the principle, so work started in converting the software without changing the functionality originally provided for DLR. The production of software for Lewisham also benefited from being produced by the much more up to date methods available for software design and safety validation by 1998. A side product of the change enabled Lewisham to be provided as an extension of an existing control area, which reduced equipment needs.

After much testing and some passenger service at low traffic times like winter weekends and after Christmas 1998, the system entered full passenger service on 20th January 1999. Upgrades have brought Lewisham into test running and to passenger service. To ensure operation would always be available during the changeover, detailed arrangements were used to keep both systems in place with secure switchover between them. The older system was decommissioned in October 1999 as it was no longer available as a fall-back option once application was made to open the Lewisham Extension to public service.

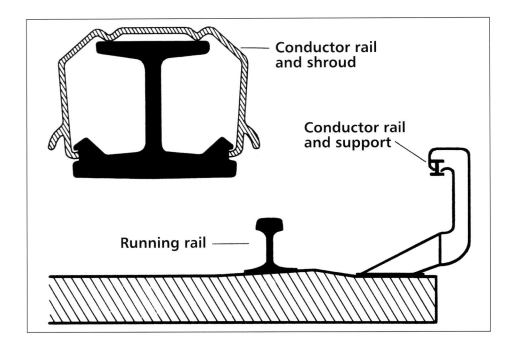

Conductor rail and shroud

Conductor rail and support

Running rail

Power supply and track

Traction current is distributed at 750V dc by means of an I-section aluminium conductor rail with a stainless steel contact surface bonded to the underside. This conductor rail is of the bottom contact type with an inverted U-section plastic shroud fitted over the top. This helps to minimise the risk of accidental electrocution and avoids the problem of snow and ice build-up associated with low-level current collection systems.

The DLR train cars are fitted with carbon collection shoes mounted on glass reinforced plastic arms, centrally-mounted on each side of the motor bogies.

DLR permanent way is standardised on the use of BS80A 80lb per year flat bottom rail laid on a mixture of ballasted and concrete trackbed forms. The Pandrol 'e' clip fastening is used on British Rail F24 type sleepers for ballasted track and a cast iron baseplate assembly on slab track. New structures and all curves of less than 100 metres radius are based on the formed concrete trackbed; other sections using traditional railway ballasting. Continuous welded rail is used throughout with alumino-thermic welds.

For the Beckton line considerable lengths of the viaduct are a trough section with ballasted track forms used within the trough. This greatly reduces the noise reflecting off the trackbed and reverberations of the structures. Concrete deck trackbed is used elsewhere with direct fixings. The ground level track is normal ballasted construction. On the Lewisham Extension, the conductor rail is of a larger cross-section, permitting the use of two sub-stations where more would have been required otherwise.

Staffing

Although the brand-new DLR gave its embryonic management team the chance to create fresh, modern staffing conditions, the smallness of the initial system brought the problem of the diseconomies of small scale.

Roughly 100 jobs were advertised in the period before opening in 1987, with over 2,200 applicants chasing the initial 54 traffic jobs. In the event, half of the successful traffic job applicants lived in the immediate Docklands area and the remainder in east London.

DLR was determined to use the benefit of automation to free staff to humanise the railway. Free from the need to drive trains staff could meet the customers, check tickets, and exert a presence in a variety of ways to oversee and aid the general running of the railway.

The formal title of the Train Captains, of which there are now 160, was firstly Traffic Assistant, because their working brief is broader than the obvious duties of DLR trains: station-based ticket inspection and passenger supervision, train fault finding and inspection, off-the-railway local community PR work and other tasks are all undertaken. This in-built flexibility is considered to have served the railway well with the basic role developing into one providing station staffing at Bank, Island Gardens, Cutty Sark, Tower Gateway and Canary Wharf as necessary. The present title is Passenger Service Agent.

Maintenance staff, understandably, have their backgrounds more firmly in railways, with many having come from the Underground or British Rail. Additionally, a variety of design, development and project management roles have been created to manage the various separate contracts whilst keeping the original railway open for business as much as possible.

The train service

The Performance Specification designed for the Initial Railway specified eight trains per hour on the two routes (Tower Gateway to Island Gardens and Stratford to Island Gardens). In fact the railway opened with six trains per hour on each service with testing to full specification taking place in 1987/88 with a view to increasing the service in 1988 to that originally planned.

The initial peak service called for 9 trains operating at 10-minute intervals on each service, and 7 trains in the off-peak every 12 minutes. An enhanced peak service using 10 trains was introduced later in 1988, with intervals of 7½ minutes scheduled on each service. At the same time, the station dwell times were reduced. The off-peak service was also increased to every 10 minutes (9 trains).

The entry into service of the P89 stock allowed a modest service increase from 5th November 1990, with 13 single-vehicle trains being scheduled. This saw the peak service improved to 6½-minute intervals, necessitating the regular use of the passing loop at Pudding Mill Lane prior to the station being built here.

From 25th February 1991, following a long period of testing, two-vehicle trains were timetabled for the first time. The teething troubles with two-vehicle operation had not been wholly overcome, however, and single vehicles on two-vehicle workings continued to operate. But the timetable saw the peak-hour services on both branches increased to 5-minute intervals with seven two-vehicle and eight one-vehicle trains scheduled on the Tower Gateway–Crossharbour and Stratford–Island Gardens services respectively. This was the first regular use of the new Crossharbour centre reversing siding, where all the two-vehicle trains had to reverse, as Mudchute and Island Gardens could still only accommodate one-vehicle trains. In fact two-vehicle operation was confined to off-peak periods to start with, as the new B90 vehicles (the first of which had arrived on 31st January 1991) were not then available for passenger service. These had started to come on stream in time for the first stage of the opening to Bank on 29th July 1991 when the Tower Gateway peak service was halved, and alternate trains diverted to operate to and from Bank, also having a 10-minute service.

All trains running to and from Bank used the westbound tunnel on a 'single line' basis initially and thus minimum reversing time was allowed. By now many two-vehicle trains were able to be operated of both P89 and B90 stock (but not of mixed types), and the peak stock requirement was for 7×2 (Bank/Tower Gateway–Crossharbour) and 8×1 (Stratford–Island Gardens). In the off peak period, each service operated every 10 minutes (Bank, Tower Gateway and Stratford), but the eight single vehicles that operated the peak Stratford service were shared between the Stratford and Tower Gateway service, the latter being extended to terminate at Island Gardens because of the shorter trains.

The completion of the eastbound running tunnel and subsequent full opening of the Bank extension on 29th November 1991 called for a total of eight two-vehicle trains in the peaks, four each on the Tower Gateway and Bank services. This enabled each service to be self-contained and the extra train catered for the additional time needed at Bank to reverse and head shunt west of the station. Total stock requirement was thus 8×2 and 8×1, 16 trains and 24 vehicles. (The proposal to run a five-minute peak service to Bank and no service at peak times to Tower Gateway was dropped at a late stage, and certainly after publicity had been made available announcing the proposal.) The off-peak service was the same as hitherto, with the Tower Gateway service operated by single vehicle trains.

Although major upgrading work had been proceeding on the Docklands Light Railway from very soon after its opening, Mudchute and Islands Gardens stations on the south leg still remained capable of accommodating one-vehicle trains only, a problem being the restricted space at Island Gardens and the possibility of the future extension under the River Thames to Lewisham, which would need new stations anyway. However, it was subsequently decided to lengthen these two stations to take two-vehicle trains and the quickest option was to close completely for a period of time, from after traffic on Friday 6th March 1992. Because of the restricted space available at Island Gardens, it was only possible to lengthen one platform (No. 2), the other being retained for single-vehicle trains only. The railway re-opened on Sunday 12th April 1992, but because of uncompleted work, two-vehicle trains could still not operate to Island Gardens until 8th June 1992.

The timetable introduced on Monday 9th March 1992 changed operating patterns and train formations considerably. This was the first use, on a regular basis, of the centre platforms at Canary Wharf for reversing purposes (where Stratford trains terminated), with Bank trains (two-vehicle) and Tower Gateway (one-vehicle) terminating at Crossharbour. With each service operating at eight-minute intervals, this called for 9×2 and 6×1 trains – 15 trains, 24 vehicles. This increased the capacity on the Stratford branch, with a two-vehicle train every eight minutes (peaks) instead of a one-vehicle train every five minutes. Both Bank and Tower Gateway gained more frequent services (every eight instead of ten minutes), although the latter was effectively reduced by the operation of one-vehicle trains instead of two. Another change was that the service operated with no reduction during the midday off-peak period. With the restoration of through services, the principles of the previous timetable continued. Requiring one extra vehicle (10×2 and 5×1) throughout the day – 15 trains, 25 vehicles – the eight-minute pattern on each service continued, although there was a changeover of operating patterns on the peak 'shoulders'.

Further timetable changes were made from 25th January 1993, to match the services provided with public demand. The peak service remained at eight-minute intervals at the same operating patterns, while that in the off-peak was reduced to ten-minute intervals and evening services (20.00 to 21.30) to every 12 minutes.

Until the original sections of the DLR were connected to Alcatel signalling, the Beckton service, from its opening on 28th March 1994, comprised a self-contained shuttle service operating from 05.20 to 21.30 on Mondays to Fridays. Between 07.00 and 19.00, five two-vehicle trains provided a 10-minute service and outside these times three trains operated an unusual 13-minute interval service.

The increasing use of the new offices around Canary Wharf saw continued increases in ridership, especially on the Bank branch. A six-minute peak service was introduced between Bank and Island Gardens from 31st May 1994 with marginal reductions on the Tower Gateway–Crossharbour service (at 8/10/12-minute intervals) and 6/8/10-minute intervals on the Stratford route. Whilst the number of trains was unchanged, the vehicle requirement was increased by one to 26.

From 3rd October 1994 late-evening services were resumed on the Initial Railway network, operating until around 00.30. The Beckton–Poplar shuttle continued to finish at 21.30.

The Bank service was further increased to 5-minute intervals in the peaks from 9th January 1995, which enabled the Tower Gateway and Stratford services to revert to even 10-minute interval services. This saw an increase in stock required to 21 trains and 38 vehicles. A minor change from 18th April 1995 saw one fewer vehicle required for service. This came about by switching the two-vehicle trains to the Tower Gateway–Crossharbour service and the single vehicle trains to the Beckton–Poplar shuttle service.

Saturday services resumed on 20th May 1995 but only between Tower Gateway and Island Gardens and between Stratford and Canary Wharf. Saturday services began around 06.00, which was half an hour later than on Mondays to Fridays. This was as a result of the additional time required for the computer system to

change over from the old to the new system. A similar service pattern on Sundays began on 25th June 1995, operating between 07.30 and 23.30. Meanwhile, the whole railway changed over to the new Alcatel signalling from 10th July 1995, with services continuing to operate on existing schedules.

Bank Station gained a Saturday service from 29th July 1995, while on Mondays to Fridays from 31st July 1995, the Beckton service was extended to Tower Gateway. This meant that for most of the day, this terminus served two routes – Island Gardens/Crossharbour and Beckton. The peak service required 22 trains and 38 vehicles. For the first time, the Beckton branch had a service after 21.30, which also operated through to Tower Gateway. During this late-evening period, the Tower Gateway–Island Gardens service was discontinued, the latter destination being served by trains from Bank.

The continued increase in numbers of passengers using Bank Station in the peaks resulted in alternate Tower Gateway–Crossharbour trains being diverted to Bank as a stop-gap measure from 30th October 1995. This reduced the service to Tower Gateway to every 20 minutes, although it was still served by the Beckton service. This meant that Bank had one additional train (making five instead of four) in each 20-minute period. The stock requirement remained unchanged.

Weekend changes saw an all-day Tower Gateway–Beckton service introduced from Saturday 16th December 1995 and, from the following day, Bank received a Sunday service for the first time.

The Docklands Light Railway network suffered a serious blow on the evening of Friday 9th February 1996, with the IRA bomb explosion near the DLR station at South Quay. Services were suspended south of Canary Wharf with four two-vehicle trains being unable to return to depot – they were outstabled at Island Gardens. A temporary timetable was introduced on Monday 12th February which provided a 5-minute service Bank–Canary Wharf, 10 minutes Stratford–Canary Wharf and Tower Gateway–Beckton and 20 minutes Tower Gateway–Blackwall. This required 17 two-vehicle trains but was reduced to 15 two-vehicle trains a week later because the Tower Gateway–Blackwall shuttles were serving no useful purpose. An improvement was made from 9th March 1996 by extending the Bank–Canary Wharf service one station on to Heron Quays. This was achieved by using the centre platform at Canary Wharf and then single line working to the 'up' platform at Heron Quays. Through services to Island Gardens resumed on 15th April 1996, using the previous full-service schedules, although South Quay station remained closed until 22nd April 1996.

Further increased services on the DLR would be dependent on the remodelling of the West India Quay delta junction. Trains used the new facilities from 27th December 1995, but on existing schedules. From 22nd April 1996, enhanced peak services were introduced. Bank had a 4-minute service but, because the single line section to Island Gardens could not accommodate such a frequent service, the service beyond Crossharbour was halved to every 8 minutes. The peak-hour Stratford and Beckton services were each improved to 8 minute intervals, while the Tower Gateway–Canary Wharf service operated every 16 minutes. This service required 26 trains and 44 vehicles. From 6th January 1997, however, the peak service between Tower Gateway and Canary Wharf was eliminated which resulted in 23 all two-vehicle trains required for service.

Peak services were increased further from 26th August 1997 with services based on a 7-minute pattern, enabling Bank to have a 3½-minute peak service. Tower Gateway continued to be served only by Beckton trains in the peak, comprising a mix of single and double vehicles. The stock requirement was thus increased to 28 trains and 52 vehicles.

With the morning peak being more concentrated than the evening, morning services were further enhanced from 20th April 1998. Bank was given a 3-minute peak service, Stratford 6 minutes, while Tower Gateway–Beckton was marginally reduced from 7 to 7½ minutes. This service called for 30 trains and 56 vehicles in service during the morning peak, but the stock requirement for the evening peak remained unaltered. The morning peak requirement for 56 vehicles (out of a fleet total of 70) proved a little optimistic and the Bank–Crossharbour morning peak service was cut back to terminate at Canary Wharf from 1st September 1998. Whilst morning peak services remained based on the 3/6-minute principle (6–9 minutes Tower Gateway–Beckton), the stock requirement became the same as for the evening peak – 28 trains, 52 vehicles.

The closure of the line south of Crossharbour for Lewisham extension work saw minor changes to service from 11th January 1999. The same service patterns applied in each peak but in the evening the Bank–Crossharbour service was cut back to Canary Wharf. This was to enable the reversing siding at Crossharbour to accommodate a reversing Stratford train and a reversing Bank train (that would have previously gone on to Island Gardens) every 7 minutes. All trains were scheduled to be formed of two vehicles, the morning peak requiring 27 trains (54 vehicles) and the evening peak 25 trains (50 vehicles).

Test running between Crossharbour and Lewisham began on 22nd August 1999 with certain trains from Bank and Stratford being extended (empty) over the new extension. Service patterns remained unchanged over the 'public' sections.

Full passenger services to Lewisham began on 20th November 1999 and the opportunity was taken to standardise both peak services. Of course, even more trains are required for service, stretching the 70-strong fleet to the limit. The new timetable requires 30 trains (60 vehicles) in both peaks, but should any stock shortfall occur, this will be applied to the Beckton route by reducing train lengths from two vehicles to one. Traffic is growing on this section of the railway but not yet to the extent which would cause an embarrassment if a single vehicle had to substitute for a double.

The current Monday to Friday services on the Docklands Light Railway can be summarised as follows:

	Peaks		Midday		Evening after 21.30	
Bank–Canary Wharf	3	} 15×2	10	} 6×2	12	} 5×2
Canary Wharf–Lewisham	6		10		12	
Stratford–Canary Wharf	6	} 7×2	10	} 5×2	15	} 2×2
Canary Wharf–Crossharbour	6		10		—	
Crossharbour–Lewisham	—		20		—	
Tower Gateway–Beckton	7½	8×2	10	6×2	15	4×2
Trains in Service:	**30×2**		**17×2**		**11×2**	

The Saturday 'busy' service (07.30 to 19.30) requires 15 trains (30 vehicles) and Sunday 'busy' (start to 19.30) 12 trains (24 vehicles).

SUMMARY OF DLR TRAINS REQUIRED FOR PEAK SERVICE

Date from	Formations		Trains	Vehicles	Notes
31.08.87	9×1	—	9	9	
26.09.88	10×1	—	10	10	
05.11.90	13×1	—	13	13	
25.02.91	8×1	7×2	15	22	
29.11.91	8×1	8×2	16	24	
09.03.92	6×1	9×2	15	24	Closure of Mudchute & Island Gardens and 8-min peak service to Bank
08.06.92	5×1	10×2	15	25	Reopening of Mudchute & Island Gardens
28.03.94	5×1	15×2	20	35	Beckton branch (shuttle) opens
31.05.94	4×1	16×2	20	36	6-minute peak service to Bank
09.01.95	4×1	17×2	21	38	5-minute peak service to Bank
10.07.95	5×1	16×2	21	37	
31.07.95	6×1	16×2	22	38	Beckton service extended to Tower Gateway
12.02.96	—	17×2	17	34	No service south of Canary Wharf because of bomb explosion at South Quay
19.02.96	—	15×2	15	30	Tower Gateway–Blackwall shuttle service in peaks discontinued
15.04.96	6×1	16×2	22	38	Full service resumed south of Canary Wharf
22.04.96	8×1	18×2	26	44	Full junction working at West India Quay and 4-minute peak service to Bank
06.01.97	—	23×2	23	46	
26.08.97	4×1	24×2	28	52	3½-minute peak service to Bank
20.04.98	4×1	26×2	30	56	3-minute peak service to Bank
01.09.98	4×1	24×2	28	52	
11.01.99	—	27×2	27	54	Closure of Mudchute & Island Gardens
20.11.99	—	30×2	30	60	Opening of Lewisham extension

Where DLR can be developed

Around the existing railway

The Docklands Light Railway has taken the title of The Regeneration Railway as it continues to achieve the results designed by the concept of a local area distributor network. On the railway now open there is continual development alongside the tracks which the railway is absorbing into ever higher passenger loads. The continuing expansion of the Canary Wharf area and the need for improved interchange with the Jubilee Line have produced an exciting new station design which had to be grafted around the operating railway. The largest land area development alongside DLR is that of the ExCel Exhibition Centre at Custom House which means that that station has to see drastic expansion to accommodate the crowds attending. This development is much needed evidence of the correctness of the decision to build the Beckton Extension in that it alone could have attracted the development and its associated employment. The University of East London Campus at Cyprus has also helped raise passenger numbers.

Developments at Shadwell for improved interchange with the East London Underground line are being investigated and if progressed could be in use in 2003. With Lewisham now open, there are developing plans towards passenger friendly local improvements adjacent to the station.

South Quay area, badly affected by terrorist bombing, is beginning to see restoration to its previous busy employment and the last area of the original Isle of Dogs low density employment development could become a 37 storey development with attendant station improvements there yet again.

New lines

DLR commissioned an 'Horizon Study' in late 1997 to look for all the potential future possibilities for expansion and the practicality of their integration into the existing railway. There are still significant transport gaps in the area in which DLR operates that could benefit from rail service and would generate benefit to the rest of the operation.

Silvertown and London City Airport

The growing importance of London City Airport is requiring access to it to be integrated into the rail network since the present passenger count of 1.5 million per annum will expand to at least 3 million by 2005. This airport has road access problems which will choke it without a DLR line serving it. Thus extensive work has progressed into achieving a preferred route. The airport alone would not be sufficiently attractive to the railway, but the areas along the river nearby are changing fast from industrial to residential and will provide the basis to go forward to a Private Public Partnership. One of the many decisions yet to be made will include connecting into North Woolwich. There will be at least passive provision for a longer term plan to extend under the river to Woolwich centre but this has to be integrated into the plans for other public transport river crossings. A Transport and Works Act application will be made in the near future.

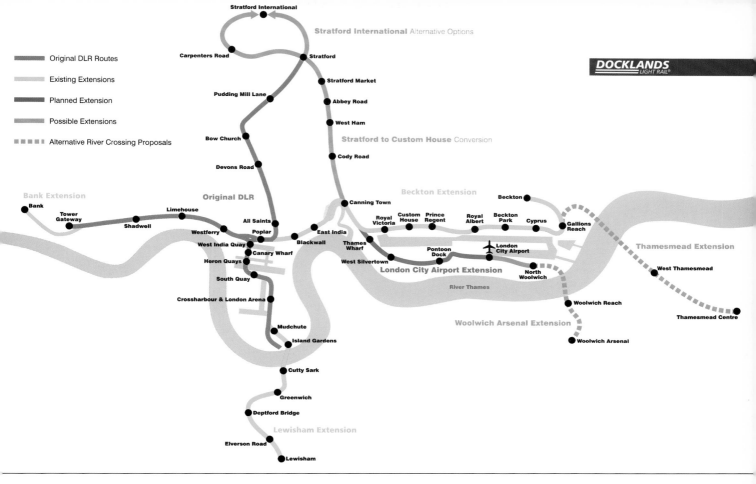

Original DLR Routes
Existing Extensions
Planned Extension
Possible Extensions
Alternative River Crossing Proposals

Stratford and Stratford International Station

With the now well-developed plans for City Airport, which will need a junction at Canning Town, and the massive redevelopment being formulated around a Stratford International Station the whole artery between these is being investigated for potential development of DLR. The new Jubilee Line has increased the already good connections at Stratford but the new International station 500m north could be served from DLR at lower cost and difficulty if the whole North London Railway down to Canning Town was incorporated into DLR. Thus plans are progressing to look at this corridor. Whilst the Underground is already there, DLR would be able to have many more stations and thus do the local distribution function it already does so well in neighbouring areas. This would be for 2007 opening or later to integrate with the International Station.

Other possibilities

These could look to a better eastern centre interchange at Barking, but would need to be integrated into development as yet unformulated. There are some other gaps in the area but all the possibilities must be viewed in the light of their impact on the already heavily used railway as much as the cost benefit to any area.

Local railway history

About three-quarters of the initial DLR system opened in 1987 re-used old railway routes. Some of these older railways had been disused for many years; others remained in service right up to the day the DLR took over the tracks. The origin, development and, in many cases, decay of these railways is closely tied up with the history of the up-river docks.

The City route

In 1836 an Act of Parliament was passed authorising the construction of 'The Commercial Railway' running from Minories, by the City Wall, 3½ miles east to Brunswick Wharf at Blackwall. The railway passed close by the Regents Canal Dock, the West India Docks and the East India Docks. The railway was not initially intended to handle freight – rather it sought to attract large numbers of passengers whose journey from London to the Docks had until then to be made either by river – slow and often circuitous – or by road, which was even slower. Before the introduction of the telegraph, all messages had to be conveyed by hand and a continuous stream of clerks, messenger boys and businessmen travelled to and from the Docks daily. Additionally, the increasing popularity of the seaside had resulted in a growing number of steamer services from London to Kent and Essex resorts – services which could operate far more cheaply and efficiently if they started from Blackwall rather than from the Pool of London.

Two rival schemes had been put before Parliament for very similar routes to the docks and the unsuccessful rivals eventually merged with the Commercial Railway, with George Stephenson and George Bidder becoming the Company's engineers. In 1839, a year after construction had started, the company received parliamentary approval for an extension from Minories to Fenchurch Street and a formal change of name to the London & Blackwall Railway.

Opening on 4th July 1840, the London & Blackwall Railway was in its day a sophisticated and rapid system. Carried mainly on a 4,020-yard viaduct – the cheapest way of building in a congested urban area – the double-tracked railway was cable-hauled using a drum-to-drum system and seven miles of hemp rope for each track, with winding engines at either end of the line.

Within two years of opening the railway had extended into the City to Fenchurch Street and was experimenting with goods traffic. It was however isolated from the rest of the growing London rail network by virtue of its wide track gauge and cable haulage, the cables having a tendency to occasionally twist or snap, despite now being metal instead of hemp. To expand further the railway needed to standardise its equipment. In 1845 parliament passed an Extension Act for the London & Blackwall Railway, authorising a connection with the Eastern Counties Railway at Bow and the change of gauge and haulage. The last cable-hauled train ran on 14th February 1849.

The Beckton route

Between Poplar and Beckton the DLR uses an all-new alignment.

Poplar to Stratford

The Eastern Counties Railway was incorporated in 1836, to run from Shoreditch to Norwich and Yarmouth. Within the London area the Eastern Counties Railway helped promote and then build the branch line from Stratford to North Woolwich in 1846/7 and had established at Stratford what was to become a major railway works. The London & Blackwall now became part of the growing Eastern Counties network, being eventually leased completely in 1865 to the Eastern Counties Railway, by now termed the Great Eastern Railway.

Other railways besides the Eastern Counties wanted to share in the lucrative docks traffic, and it was through a rival company, the North London Railway, that the DLR section from Bow Church to All Saints came to be built. The North London Railway (NLR) started in 1846 as the East & West India Docks and Birmingham Junction Railway Company. The intention was to build a freight line linking the docks with the London to Birmingham line at Chalk Farm in north London. It took four years to build and open the line as far south as Bow, and it was not until 1851 that the railway reached Poplar. Poplar Dock was served by a large goods depot and an extensive yard of sidings with over 14 miles of track. Part of this area is now occupied by the DLR Operations and Maintenance Centre.

Passing through some of the more prosperous new suburbs of London, the railway company carried passengers from the start, although it was not until 1866 that passenger services extended south of Bow. The heyday of the North London Railway occurred in the last twenty years of the 19th century. Over its Poplar line ran three other major railway companies' freight trains, and around Poplar Docks were grouped huge warehouses.

West India Quay to Lewisham

In complete contrast to the NLR was the tiny neighbouring Millwall Extension Railway, the route of which is now used by the DLR from Crossharbour to Island Gardens. It began back in 1865 when construction work started on the Millwall Dock. Millwall Dock was built with an internal rail network, designed around horse-hauled wagons – steam locomotives were too much of a fire risk with quaysides of wooden ships, often with canvas sails.

At around the same time, the Great Eastern Railway and the Millwall Canal Company (owners of the Millwall Dock) jointly proposed a railway which would develop the southern part of the Isle of Dogs. Running south from Millwall Junction at the top of the Isle of Dogs, the line would skirt the east side of West India Docks and pass alongside the Millwall Dock to terminate on the bank of the Thames close by the jetty for the ferry to Greenwich.

Although this railway, the Millwall Extension Railway, would benefit its promoters, the neighbouring East & West India Docks saw the line as a threat, abstracting traffic, and they objected vigorously. Thus it was that the Millwall Extension Railway, single track throughout, took six years to build, opening in 1871 to Millwall Docks and in 1872 to North Greenwich Station situated above the present-day Island Gardens Station. The DLR between Mudchute and Lewisham follows a route new to railway operation.

DLR Route Map

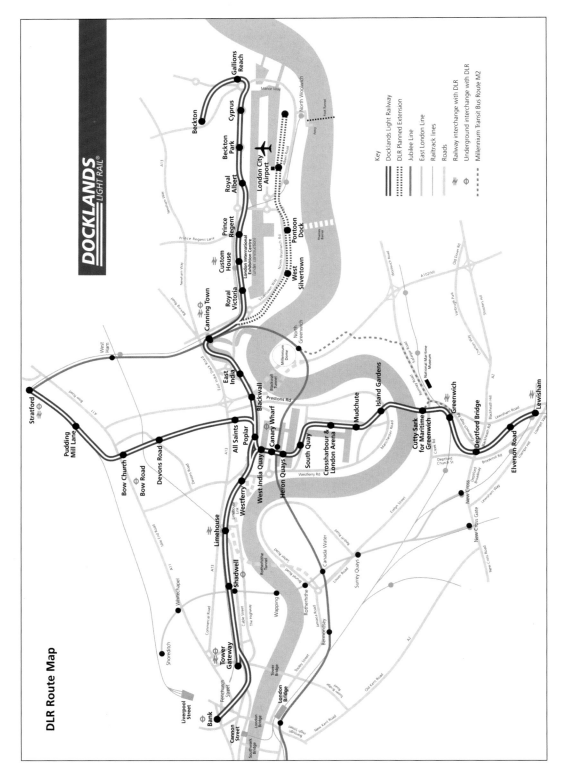